HATTERSLEY

THE OLD AND THE

Thorncliff House, early 1900's. It was situated next to the New Inn on Mottram Road. The last resident was Mr Bradley who was a manager at Wall's Factory in nearby Godley.

MARGARET KNOTT.

Author's Note

To many the name Hattersley is associated with either an M.P. and author, who likes soap operas, particularly Coronation Street, or a place somewhere in the north that was the scene of horrific child murders in 1965. Those responsible, Myra Hindley and Ian Brady, may have made this suburb of Hyde, formerly in Cheshire infamous; but many residents of Tameside know it as the place in which they grew up. Others will remember moving into this country area from various parts of Manchester in the sixties and early seventies. Still others, like myself, will know it as a green and pleasant oasis, where cattle and poultry roamed freely on farmland. It was a place where wild flowers and crops grew in meadows and fields smelled sweetly of fresh cut hay. Children on their bikes would free-wheel down the lanes.In this book, I've tried to show some of the farms and cottages that were demolished in 'Old" Hattersley and also the stages of building the 'New" Hattersley. For those who rember the old, I hope it's a trip down memory lane, and for those who don't I hope you will value an insight into the history of this township in Photographs.

Published by Foxline Publishing
32, Urwick Road, Romiley, Stockport. SK6 3JS

Janey Manifold of Pingot Farm. c.1940.

Introduction.

The name Hattersley is derived from Addersley, meaning the field of adders. The manor of Hattersley was originally held by the Stokeports under the earldom. There is a record of a mesne manor held here by a family of the local name, represented by Ralph de Hatterslegh in the thirteenth century. Isabel, the daughter of Sir Richard de Stokeport held lands at Hatterslegh. The Stokeport interest passed to the Warrens of Poynton; later the principal estates became vested in the Carringtons. Their daughter Jane married George Booth and so the estates were carried to the Booth family of Dunham. Later lands passed to the Earls of Stamford and Warrington.

In 1858 Lord Stamford disposed of the manor to John Chapman of Hill End, Mottram, then in 1899 it passed to his son Edward Chapman. A Saxon corn mill once formed an important feature of the township of Hattersley. The Saxons also carried on smelting operations in Werneth, getting fuel for the work from the forests of Hatersley. The forests are said to have been most extensive and fragments of charcoal have been found there.

Dedication

I dedicate this book to all who lived in Hattersley and especially in memory of my lovely mum, Janey Manifold, the youngest daughter born at Pingot Farm, Hattersley in 1914 and tragically died from cancer in 1965.

Hattersley
by Mrs M Stone.

A Grand new life was to be our fate
When we moved from town to Hattersley estate.
This lovely place so clean and bright,
The Kids were filled with sheer delight.
We planted flowers, trees and shrubs
In gardens, borders and in tubs.
Deep roots were laid and new friends made
In this new found leafy glade.
It's now two decades and more
Since we arrived here, so unsure
Of what to find, yet time has shown
Our love for this fair place has grown.
The glorious scenery and gorgeous view
Yet, we remain Mancunians true,
Never wanted to belong to Hyde,
Perhaps it's right they chose Tameside.

Harrop Edge c.1965. A view taken from the skyscraper flats on Underwood Road, looking towards Harrop Edge. Mottram Road runs from the bungalow on the left to just above the flat roof of the building on the right of the photograph. The older building with the two chimneys to the right of centre is Marl Villa on Mottram Road. A close-up can be found on Page No.25.

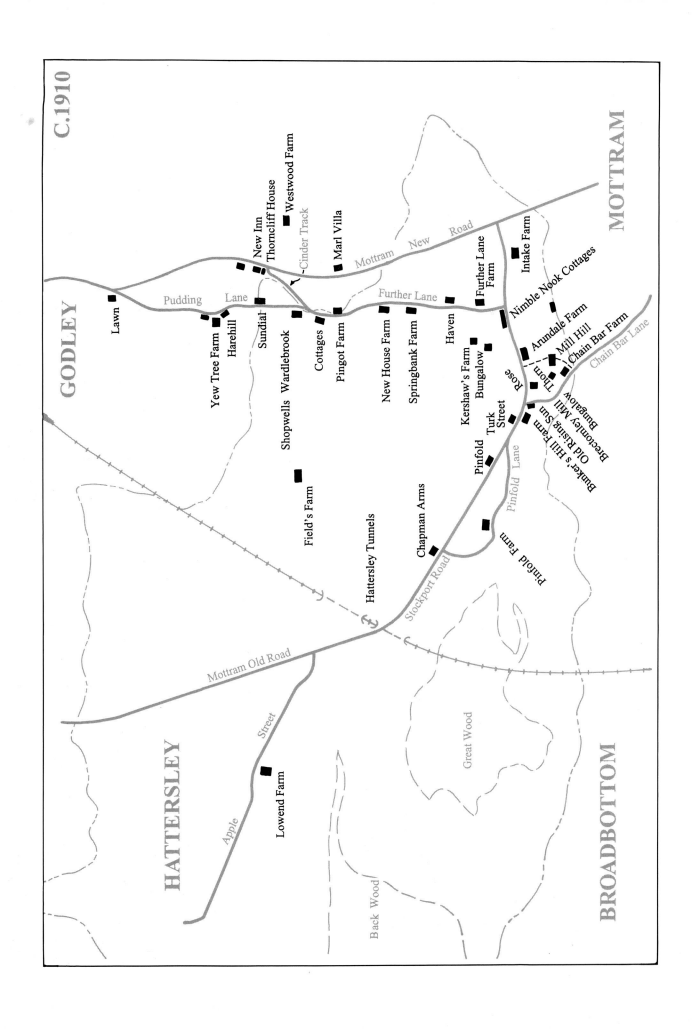

(left). **The New Inn, Mottram Road 1993.** This Inn was first licensed around 1856 with Robert Turner being the first innkeeper. One famous landlord was Sam Swann, who was regarded as a 'strong giant' as he could easily crush a pint pot in his hands. He later went on to keep the Chapman Arms in Hattersley. As the new overspill estate took shape the inn changed from a country pub, catering for walkers and cyclists, to be the 'local' for thousands of new residents. The garages were knocked down and the pub was extended. Just lower than the New Inn was a wooden bungalow, where Mr & Mrs Horn and their son Leslie lived.

(below). **Hattersley c.1955.** This photograph appeared on the cover of the Parish magazine of St.Barnabas' church at the time of the parish Jubilee in 1988. At the time the question was asked as to the location. If that was never answered, then here is the explanation. The farm on the left is Pingo: Farm and the cottages in the centre are all on Further Lane, now Underwood Road. The house to the right is Wardlebrook Farm at the start of Pudding Lane. The picture was taken from land to the left of the New Inn just off a lane known as the Cinder Track.

Manchester Public Libraries.

The Hattersley News

Price 16p or £1.75 annually   MID-NOVEMBER, 1988

HATTERSLEY THIRTY YEARS AGO

We would be interested to know the name of the lane in front of the cottage to the right of the photograph and any other thoughts on the topography.

We have a sketch map dated 1794 which shows the location of Hattersley but there is no sign of Hyde! We at Hattersley are pleased to welcome the new comers at Hyde and hope that they will fit in well with their neighbours in ancient Hattersley.

An added attraction for Hattersley folk is that within a few minutes walk we can be in the open country. And if you want a village atmosphere where everybody knows everybody you need travel no further than our shopping areas; there is always someone to pass the time of day with us.

We have the best of both worlds.

Parish Silver Jubilee
1963 — 1988
25 Years of Service to God and People

(top). The Parish Magazine of St.Barnabas Church, Hattersley, at the time of the Silver Jubilee in 1988. The vicar at the time was Canon John E.Bowers who was a keen cyclist. He did a great deal of good among the community in Hattersley along with his colleagues in the other churches on the estate. He cycled from Lands End to John 'o' Groats to raise money for the church.

Hattersley Today

(see map below)

A- Underwood Road
B- Hattersley Road West
C- Hattersley Road East
D- Chain Bar Road
E- Ashworth Lane
F- Field's Farm Road
G- Bunker's Hill Road
H- Arundale Close/Grove/School
I- Further Lane
J- Wardlebrook Avenue
K- Sundial Wlk/Close
L- Pudding Lane
M- Harehill Road
N- Chapman Road

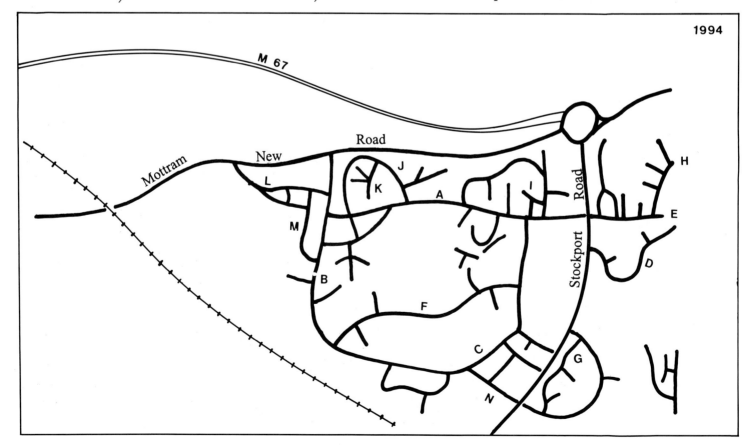

(top). **Westwood Farm, Matley.** Built c.1840 it was situated across the road from the New Inn, up a short lane off Mottram road facing Hattersley. Mr Edwin Foulkes, his wife, sixteen year old son Gordon and thirteen year old daughter Betty lived there when tragedy struck in 1944. On the morning of Christmas Eve; whilst the family were in bed a flying bomb, known as a 'Doodlebug' came over from the Manchester air raids and struck their home. Post Office workers in Stalybridge saw the bomb coming and ducked under the counters. The blast was heard as far away as Dukinfield. Cinders from a lane were blown into the door of the New Inn, and the roof was blown off. Windows of Springbank Farm on Further Lane and Harehill on Pudding Lane were shattered. Westwood was badly damaged as were the cottages behind the farm.

(bottom). Betty was sleeping in the front bedroom with her grandmother, Elizabeth Greenwood, who had come from Failsworth to stay for Christmas. The whole of the bedrooms collapsed to ground level and Betty's brother Gordon and his grandmother were killed. Edwin and his wife escaped with cuts and eye problems and Betty, although deafened, remarkably escaped with cuts. Six cattle in the shippon were killed and the pony used to deliver milk had to be destroyed. The following day other relatives arrived for Christmas only to find this scene of devastation.

THE LANE that ran from the New Inn to the bottom of Further Lane. Pictured top is Stanley Manifold of Springbank Farm in the 1950's. He used to clear this path of snow each winter. Cinders were often scattered from the open fires in the houses, to fill in potholes and to prevent people slipping. It become known to many in Hattersley as the Cinder Track. In the distance is Pingot Farm.

Below is the gate and stile at the junction with Further Lane which ran to the left and Pudding Lane that went right. The Hyde/Mottram boundary was originally near this Gate. Most of Pudding Lane was in Godley, and Further Lane was Hattersley. With the help of the map on Page 4 each dwelling mentioned in the book can be located.

Sundial Cottage, Pudding Lane. Built 1697 and named after the sundial between the upper windows, this was Hattersley's only listed building and due to severe vandalism, it could not be saved. The last resident was Stanley Hall, pictured here with his dog in the 1950's.

A derelict Sundial with cranes showing the start of building the new Hattersley. From 1961-1966, Wellington Excavation & Haulage from Knotty Ash in Liverpool, worked on the new roads and sewers on the Hyde side of Hattersley.

Sundial Close 1993. The name Sundial lives on in Sundial Close and Sundial Walk. The new Pudding Lane follows the original line of the old lane.

Sundial Walk 1993.

Pudding Lane in 1993.

Pudding Lane near Harehill Farm looking towards Harrop Edge. Westwood Farm that was bombed, can be seen on the left of the picture near the gate. It is thought that a pub existed on Pudding Lane in the 18th century called the Blacksmith's Arms. In 1781 the landlord was John Turner. c.1850 it became known as the Horseshoe before closing in 1880. Trail Hunts met at the pub. In 1878 the winner of the trail hunt was 'Bloomer' owned by Nathan Lees and a copper kettle was the prize.

On Pudding Lane, near Yew Tree Farm there were two cottages and at the Godley end of the lane is the red brick house known as THE LAWN. Mr Stansfield, who built Hyde Hippodrome lived there after Mr Wilkinson. At the Hattersley end of the lane was another brick building (see Page 5) known originally as Shopwells and later as Wardlebrook.. The Smith family lived there. The name lives on today in Wardlebrook Avenue.

(above). **Bessie Clayton** in Church Girls Brigade uniform outside Harehill Farm with YEW TREE FARM, owned by Alfred Hill, to the right.

Harehill Farm, Pudding Lane, Godley. c.1960. Owned by the Clayton family, it was originally built in 1669 and twice extended in the 1700's to make two homes. Today Harehill Road runs parallel to the beginning of Hattersley Road West.

Tameside Local Studies

Cottages at the Hyde end of Further Lane. c.1950's. A Wheelwright, Fred Jones lived in the lower cottage and a lady who kept chickens lived in the top one. It is thought that she used the cellar to chop off their heads. At one time a Mr Harrop lived here. He was killed on Mottram Road whilst going for water to the New Inn.

The same cottages now ready for demolition. The former residents of Hattersley had to vacate their properties by November 1960. Seen in the photograph is the author of this book and her mother who was born at Pingot Farm, seen on the right. Most of the farms and cottages in Hattersley had outdoor toilets that were emptied by the local corporation once each week. Even in an area where farm smells were common this job was done late in the evening when residents were indoors. The men were named 'Midnight Mechanics'. The wooden building with the small window could have housed one such toilet. Usually, a bucket type bin was below a box with a hinged lid with one or more holes. Large families could go in pairs. Sheets of torn up newspaper often hung on a nail behind the door.

Pingot Farm, Further Lane, owned by the Manifold family. William and Hannah had seven children, William, Raymond, Stanley, Ben, Twins Ruth and Mary and Janey. Seen here from the rear c.1940, later it was divided into two smaller cottages to accomodate married sons and their families.

Mary and Janey with 'Bonnie' and two young evacuees from Lowestoft. The girls were staying at the home of Janey and her Husband in Hadfield. They came to Hattersley to help the war effort on the land. Ironically, Westwood Farm that was flattened by a bomb in 1944, was only a short distance away from Pingot Farm which was considered a safe place well away from the city centre of Manchester that was badly damaged during the Second World War. A telegram arrived for one of the girls. It wrongly said, 'Mother's dead, come home at once'. It should have read, 'Mother said, come home at once.'

William Manifold senior, cutting corn and making stooks at Pingot Farm. Corn stooks were made up of eight sheaves, four on each side made them stand up to dry. This picture was taken in the early 1940's and the gable end of the Sundial cottage can be seen on the right, in the distance.

Making sheaves, from corn in the field across from the two cottages on Further Lane. William Manifold and daughters Janey and Mary.

Sisters Ruth and Janey and Janey's Husband Harry. c.1940.

Cutting Hay at Pingot Farm c.1940. Janey and Mary and a helper, assisted by "Bonnie' are under the direction of William Manifold. Up until 1970 a man and his daughter came to Hattersley each year to help on the farm as casual labour. They were very clean and pushed a large pram containing all their belongings. Each night they slept in the lanes and fields with their heads inside the upturned pram to keep dry, with their belongings under a tarpaulin.

(above). **Pingot Farm c.1960.** Seen here ready for demolition.

(right). **Pingot Farm** has been demolished but the huge barn is still standing. c.1960.

Pingot Farm 1960. The farm has been demolished and the barn is partially down.

The author of this book c.1960 This shows the size of the huge barn at Pingot Farm. It was in here that one of the sons, Ben, tragically lost his life in the thirties.

Pingot Farm finally gone. The photograph on the front cover of this book is taken from the same spot.

After demolition, a silver birch tree was all that remained near Pingot Farm. The Sundial cottage can just be seen in the distance on the left.

Taken in the early sixties, this is the same location, the tree is still there as is the Sundial Cottage. The new Hattersley had begun off Underwood Road. The local paper first announced in 1962 that there was a scheme to build 990 dwellings and one year later that Hattersley were to have skyscraper flats. At first the new residents remember how windy it was and until the gardens were set out, many had to leave their doors on wooden planks. One lady remembers a cow walking up a plank to her front door. It was obviously confused by all the houses appearing in its pasture.

Underwood Road 1993.

Underwood Road 1993.

Building Underwood Court flats, looking towards Harrop Edge. c.1965. The houses are on Underwood Road. A lady who lived at the top of one of the towerblocks and looked out onto the rolling hills thought it was lovely. She is reported in the Manchester Evening News as telling her friends that she lives in the Hattersley Hilton. Many of the other residents were soon to disagree with her. Their walls were full of condensation and the pylons prevented the televisions working properly.

Hattersley Road West - Top left. Fields Farm Road - right. The building of these houses by Wimpey's were started c.1962. The first people moved onto the estate in May 1963 from Wythenshawe, Gorton, Ardwick, Cheetham Hill and Hulme. They were welcomed by the Mayor of Hyde and Wall's meat company in Godley gave them sausages and a local milk round gave them free milk. The railway station is now to the right of Sandybank Court, towerblock on Hattersley Road West. The first bus service was the number 5 from Hyde, but as this was not very frequent, local delivery men gave residents lifts into Hyde. The newcomers had varying reactions to this country place. They liked the fresh air, the snow and the wildlife, but they missed the corner shops, the buses and the cinemas. Until shops were opened on Sandybank Avenue, mobile shops served the 1157 families. The Manchester Evening News reported in August 1964, 'overspills are making headlines everywhere, Hattersley has got 4,000 people, 2 pubs, 3 wooden churches, one doctor, no cinemas, no playgrounds and almost no teenage entertainment.'

The view up Further Lane. c.1955 Pingot Farm on the left.

The rear view of Pingot Farm shortly before demolition. One of the trees to the right of the picture was a pear tree and was known to everyone who lived nearby for its abundant crop each year. To the far left is the gable end of New House Farm, owned by Stanley Hall who also lived at the Sundial Cottage.

On Further Lane and up from New House Farm was **Springbank Farm**, seen here from the back. It was owned by Stanley Manifold who had two sons, Graham and Malcolm. This was taken in the 1950's as Father watches his son on the Fordson Standard Tractor. Manchester Corporation had plans as early as 1953 to build on the land at Hattersley. A public enquiry was held in 1957 and the plans for building houses were approved in the same year, despite a petition against it collected on Hyde Market in 1956.

Late 1950's. The field opposite Springbank Farm looking down Further Lane towards Hyde.

(above). **c.1955.** Stanley Manifold and sister Janey at Springbank Farm. The hencote is to the left and the bungalow on the right was known as the Haven.

(right). **Mrs Mason** inside her home. She lived at the red brick bungalow (to the right of the picture below) until she died at the age of 96.

(Below). **Across the fields** from Further Lane Farm could be seen **Kershaws Farm**, the white building to the left. The last farmer was Mr Rothwell, who kept pigs and hens. The brick building on the right was simply known as **The Bungalow**. The last resident was a sign writer who had two sons, Andrew and Geoffrey.

Further Lane Farm was towards the top of the lane named after it. The last resident was Tom Procter, who kennelled hounds for the North East Cheshire drag hunt. Today there is a Further Lane just off the top of Underwood Road near Stockport Road. This photograph shows the author's brother and was taken in August 1960.

Marl Villa on Mottram Road, Matley 1993. This house is higher up the road from Westwood and is almost in line from where Pingot farm was situated on Hattersley. Mottram road was cut c.1836, previously the road from Mottram to Hyde was down through Further Lane and Pudding Lane.

Start of the building on the Mottram side of Hattersley. The roads and sewers on this side were done by James O'Grady and Company. This site was once used by Mottram Show and is now the area near the Longdendale Recreation Centre.

These houses were built by 'Boot'. Many new residents were upset by waterlogged lawns, acres of mud, bulldozers and concrete mixers. In 1963 they held a public meeting in Pinfold school to air their grievances. In 1964 the Manchester Evening News commented that 'Hattersley is slowly developing and one day it will be a nice place, but travel is poor, there's overcrowding in the school and families feel disowned by Manchester Corporation. Some call it "The Isle of Nothing". There are many lonely women at home with young children and teens are bored with nothing to do.'

Mottram Show (c.1950's), which started in 1904 used to be held in the fields below Ashworth Lane on the Mottram side of Hattersley. This picture shows the Grand Parade when the prize winners collect their trophies. There used to be a large wooden stand to view the show under cover as well as benches around the main arena. Notice the commissionaire in the hut at the gate and Mottram church in the background.

Mottram Show. Exhibiters have always travelled from afar as well as locally. Here we see a trophy for the best beast in the show being presented to the owner from Hoghton near Preston. One of the attractions of the show, was the showing of pigs and their freshly washed piglets, but due to foot and mouth disease pigs were not allowed to be moved from the farms to be exhibited in shows.

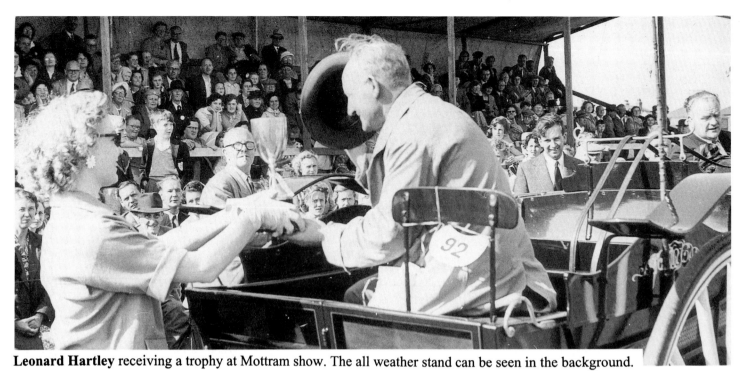

Leonard Hartley receiving a trophy at Mottram show. The all weather stand can be seen in the background.

Frances Lockett presenting a trophy at the show in 1930. She lived in Queen Street, Hyde and worked at a cotton mill called James Ashton, which was near Newton Mill on Ashton Road in Hyde. She was crowned the first Cotton Queen of Great Britain and was Miss Glossop and Hyde when she won the title in Blackpool in 1930. A waltz was written in her honour and handkerchiefs were made with her picture on them. She travelled promoting British Cotton and was treated locally as a real queen. She married in 1937 and died aged 83 in May 1993.

1950's. Working sheep dog displays were always a major part of the show. Here we see a line up at prize giving time. Second on the right is local man John Mason; the photograph was taken outside the members enclosure.

Children from Hadfield watching the show c.1959. From the left are Gillian Metcalfe and her two sisters and Pat Lounds and her brother John.

Old Farm Vehicles abandoned in a field off Further Lane as the farms were vacated. A sad reminder of days gone by. The farms were bought under compulsory purchase and the farmers and residents were fully compensated for the loss of their dwellings, but I'm sure many shed tears as they saw their life's work come to an end.

This picture was taken from the old Chapman Arms, looking towards Hyde. The work had just started on a new road seen on the left. The lorry was owned by the haulage contractors, Wellington, who laid the new sewers and roads for the estate. **Fields Farm** can just be seen to the right of the tree. The sign by the tree says 'Private Road. No Parking.'

Nimble Nook Cottages. A row of six cottages that stood on Stockport Road near the junction with Underwood Road. This photograph showing a mother and five of her children was taken at the end of the 19th century. In the distance, on the opposite side of the road is Arundale farm.

Tameside Local Studies Library

Stockport Road. The original CHAPMAN ARMS, seen on the right of the picture, was demolished in 1967. In the early 19th century it was a farmhouse and didn't open as a licensed house until c.1855. Three years later the Earl of Stamford and Warrington, who was Lord of the Manor sold the inn and land to John Chapman who gave it the name. In 1920, Robinson's brewery bought it from private owners. The new Chapman Arms was built a short distance away in 1969. Today Chapman Road is off Stockport Road. The white building in the distance is Bunker's Hill Farm. These cottages opposite the Chapman Arms were small 'starter Homes'. Having only '2 up and 2 down' they were ideal for those just married. Until modernised one still had an earth floor.

Bunker's Hill Farm, Stockport Road. Owned by Tom Taylor. The last resident was Mary Taylor.

(above). **In 1841** there were 103 houses in Hattersley and 610 inhabitants. In 1919 the year after the end of the first World War, Harold Chapman laid on a party for the people of Hattersley to celebrate the Armistice. A marquee was erected on the bowling green of the Chapman Arms. Food, drink and games for the children were all provided by Mr Chapman. Some of those present include :-Phyllis, Arthur, Emma, Eliza and Kathleen Cowley, George, William and Herbert Hadfield, Nora Harrison, Elsie and Harvey Bromley, Alice and Ethel Taylor, Alice and Arnold Parkey, Harold Roebuck, George Parkin, Mary Massey, Margery, James, Peggy and Kitty Bolt, Eddie and Joe Shaw, Ivy Lax, May, Albert and Lillian Beaver, Jessie Bennett, Arnold Bellis, Ruby Salter, Amy and Hilda Holt, Edith Hall, Alice Taylor. Not all the residents of Hattersley attended the party, with animals to feed and milk, some families rarely left their farms.

Some of the men at the Armistice Party.

Some of the ladies at the Armistice Party.

The cottages on Turk Street, also known as School Lane. Between the walls in the centre of the picture was the well. The natural spring bubbled up through the sandy soil and not only did it supply the cottages behind but also **Fields Farm** nearby. **Pinfold Farm** and the **Chapman Arms** are in the distance. The single storey buildings were used for hat planking. This was the rough shape for the hatting trade. Small fibres of rabbit fur were formed into a thin layer in a triangular shape called a batt. Two of these were worked together to form a conical hood. The hoods were then brought to the planking kettle where four to eight hardwood planks were arranged around an iron cauldron of boiling water to which a wineglass of vitriol (sulphuric acid) had been added. By constant dipping and working the hood with a planking pin (a long shaped piece of sycamore wood) it was shrunk to the size required. These were probably passed on to one of the hatting manufacturers in Stockport of which there were over 30 in 1892. This cottage industry died out due to the decline in the hatting trade from 1945.

Bunkers Hill Farm on Stockport Road and the Cottages on Turk Street. c.1960. In the 1800's William and Hannah Poolescott from Preston opened a school in Turk Street and it became known as School Lane. In 1898 the Cowley family moved into the middle cottage.

Tameside Local Studies Library

(left). Phyllis Cowley haymaking at Bunker's Hill Farm. c.1945. The white building to the right is Kershaw's Farm, next to it is the bungalow where Annie Hibbertson lived. In the distance on the left is Chain Bar Farm. As a child, Miss Cowley remembers collecting a pebble from the brooks and streams, called Red Raddle. It was used like a donkey stone for cleaning the steps. Along with other children wild plants like wood betony and yarrow were collected and sold to a herbalist in Hyde for a few coppers. The plants were made up into remedies to help with ladies problems.   *Tameside Local Studies Library.*

(below). Taken from Bunker's Hill Farm looking across to the farms on Further Lane. Kershaw's Farm is the white building on the right. Harrop Edge is the hill in the distance.   *Tameside Local Studies Library.*

Fred Robinson, looking towards Kershaw's Farm from Bunker's Hill Farm. The name Bunker's Hill lives on today on Bunker's Hill Road off Stockport Road. *Tameside Local Studies Library.*

The Pinfold. c.1969. The Pinfold was a stone walled square for stray animals. It was in the Brectomley Mill area of Hattersley. The owners of animals had to pay to get them back from the Pinfold. In the area near to the Pinfold there once stood the Stamford Arms. In 1857 the licensee was Joseph Swann and later in 1864 it was John Thomas. Bunker's Hill Farm is on the right of the picture. *Tameside Local Studies Library.*

The whole of this area on Stockport Road was known as **Brectomley Mill, Hattersley.** The gable end on the right of the photograph is the **Old Rising Sun**. A public house that dated back to the 18th century, when the first innkeeper was Samuel Smith. The last landlord was Jeremiah Smith but it was owned by Edward Chapman of Hill End in Mottram. It became known as Brook House and now it has been renovated and is known as the Manor House, a private dwelling on Chain Bar Lane. Above on the right is **Arundale Farm**. Moving to the left is **Mile End** just peeping out behind the tree. At the top left is the **Toll Bar** and to the right of it is **Chain Bar Farm**. Below is **Rose Cottage** and **Thorn Cottage** and in front of these is **The Bungalow**.

Tameside Local Studies Library.

Chain Bar Lane 1993.

Hattersley Railway Station 1993.

(below). **c.1957.** On the Mottram side of the Hattersley Road bridge is Stockport Road, which leads to the roundabout on the Mottram to Hyde road. This picture shows the junction of these roads when it was known as **Four Lane Ends**. The farm on the extreme left is **Intake Farm**. The next building to the right is **Arundale Farm**, whose name lives on in Arundale Close/Walk and Schools. Next on the right are **Nimble Nook Cottages** and far right is **Further Lane Farm**. Near to Arundale was a small farm and two cottages called **Mill Hill**.

The Manchester Public Libraries.

This bridge carrying Mottram Old Road over the Manchester to Sheffield railway line came about as a result of the decision to open out the two Hattersley Tunnels. Between 1928 and 1931, work to remove the cover from above the tunnels resulted in great amounts of spoil being deposited on the Broadbottom side of Great Wood, creating furrows which can still be seen adjacent to the railway. In 1960, the foundation of one of the bridge piers failed, resulting in closure of the road whilst repairs were carried out. The local newspapers ran several stories on progress of the work until completion some twelve months later.

The same bridge 1993. Just past the bridge on Mottram Old Road, is Apple Street, which leads down to Lowend Farm owned by the Cheetham family. This farm and the area past the Great Wood and Bothams Hall Wood to Broadbottom are all in the Hattersley boundary.

Hattersley Library April 1993. The library was originally in Pinfold School and then a trailer library was sponsored by Cheshire County Libraries. This was based at Bredbury and was pulled to Hattersley by a Land Rover. It was parked outside the doctor's surgery on Hattersley Road East. The local paper reported in 1967 that Hyde Corporation were asked to pay more towards its upkeep. In January 1973 the present library, on Kingston Arcade, was opened as a joint venture between the two authorities. In 1974 Tameside Metropolitan Borough council took over the running of the library.

Pinfold School. Opened 1967.

I N D E X.

Acknowledgement

My thanks to friends, family, Tameside Local Studies Library, work colleagues and anyone who has helped in the production of this book.